Japanese Vocabulary for JLPT N5

Master the Japanese Language Proficiency Test N5

Clay & Yumi Boutwell

Copyright © 2018 Clay Boutwell

All rights reserved.

ISBN-13: 978-1548612290
ISBN-10: 1548612294

WANT A FREE BOOK (or three)?

Get your copy of **Kanji 100 absolutely free** today.

That includes the Kindle, ePub, PDF versions. We'll even included all the MP3s for all the examples found in the book.

Simply go to http://www.TheJapanShop.com and click on "**GET MY FREE BOOK**" today!

INTRODUCTION

Taking the Japanese Language Proficiency Test is a great way to not only assess your Japanese skills, but also to give yourself a concrete goal for your studies. I am a firm believer in setting goals. It is the quickest way to make progress.

Unfortunately, with goal-setting, there is usually a problem maintaining motivation. By paying money and making plans to sit in a test (usually) in a different city, however, you are making a major investment of time and money. There are few pressures in life that can motivate better than time or money. That's why I always recommend signing up and studying for the JLPT for any serious student of Japanese.

FORMAT OF THIS BOOK

This book is essentially a glorified vocabulary list. However, every single vocabulary word found in these pages have an example sentence. Also, each word or example has a corresponding MP3 so you can be sure about the pronunciation. There are over 1,440 of these sound files.

In addition, there are "chapter" MP3s which include the Japanese vocabulary word, the example sentence, and then the English translation of the sentence. We put these eight MP3s together so you can listen while driving, while walking the dog, or while going through the book.

The chapters in the book correspond with the chapter MP3s. Each are between 10 to 15 minutes long and can be used with or without the book.

ABOUT CLAY & YUMI

Yumi was a popular radio DJ in Japan for over ten years. She has extensive training in standard Japanese pronunciation which makes her perfect for creating these language instructional audio files.

Clay has been a passionate learner of Japanese for twenty years now. He started his free language learning website, www.TheJapanesePage.com, way back in 1999 as a way to help other learners of Japanese as well as himself.

In 2002, he and Yumi opened www.TheJapanShop.com as a way to help students of Japanese get hard-to-find Japanese books. Since then, they have written over twenty books on various Japanese language topics.

Yumi and I are **very grateful** for your purchase and we truly hope this book will help you improve your Japanese. **We love our customers and don't take a single one of you for granted.** If you have any questions about this book or Japanese in general, I invite you to contact me below by email or on social media.

Clay & Yumi Boutwell (and Makoto & Megumi)
clay@thejapanshop.com

Support us on Patreon for even more goodies!
https://www.patreon.com/TheJapanesePage

http://www.TheJapanShop.com
http://www.TheJapanesePage.com

P.S. Please see the last page of the book to find the download link for the MP3s of these stories free of charge.

CONTENTS

Contents

INTRODUCTION	iv
Chapter 1	1
Chapter 2	7
Chapter 3	17
Chapter 4	31
Chapter 5	43
Chapter 6	58
Chapter 7	80
Chapter 8	98
Download Link	114

Chapter 1

【ああ】 ah; ohh
ああ、かわいいいぬ。　Ohh, what a cute dog.

【あう】 to meet
今日、友達に会います。　I will meet a friend today.

【あおい】 blue
海は、青い。　The sea is blue.

【あかい】 red
あの車は赤い。　That car is red.

【あかるい】 bright
まどから明るい光がさしてきました。　Bright light beamed through the window.

【あき】Fall

秋が来ました。Fall has come.

【あく】to open

ドアが開いた。 The door is open.

【あげる】to give

プレゼントを上げる。 (I'll) give a present.

【あさ】morning

朝が来ました。 The morning has come.

【あさごはん】breakfast

朝ごはんを食べます。 (I) eat breakfast.

【あさって】day after tomorrow

あさって、東京に行きます。 Day after tomorrow, I will go to Tokyo.

【あし】foot; leg

あの人は、足が大きいです。That person has big feet.

【あした】tomorrow

明日は、雨が降るでしょう。Tomorrow should

be rainy.

【あそこ】over there
あそこにおもちゃがあります。 There is a toy over there.

【あそぶ】to play
公園で遊びましょう。Let's play at the park.

【あたたかい】warm
今日は、暖かいです。 Today is warm.

【あたま】head
あの子は、頭がいい。 That child is very smart.

【あたらしい】new
新しい本が読みたいです。 I'd like to read a new book.

【あちら】over there
Aさんは、あちらにいますよ。 Mr. A is over there.

【あつい】hot (weather)
日本の夏は、暑いです。 Summer in Japan is hot.

【あつい】 hot (temperature)

このお茶は、まだ熱いです。This tea is still hot.

【あつい】 thick

この本は、厚いです。This book is thick.

【あっち】 over there

あっちに猫がいます。There is a cat over there.

【あと】 later

夫は、あとから来ます。My husband will come later.

【あなた】 you

あなたからどうぞ。 Please go first. (You first, please)

【あに】 older brother

この人は、私の兄です。 That person is my (older) brother.

【あね】 older sister

姉は、もうすぐ結婚します。 My (older) sister will marry soon.

Japanese Vocabulary for JLPT N5

【あの】 that
あの家がほしい。 I want that house.

【アパート】 apartment
アパートでは犬は飼えません。 At (my) apartment, dogs are not allowed. (Can't keep a dog)

【あびる】 to bathe (in water)
シャワーを浴びます。 (I'll) take a shower.

【あぶない】 dangerous
急に道に飛び出したら、危ない。 It is dangerous if you rush out into the street suddenly.

【あまい】 sweet
このチョコレートは、甘いです。 This chocolate is sweet.

【あまり】 not very (with a negative sentence)
この話は、あまりおもしろくない。 This story isn't very interesting.

【あめ】 rain
明日は、雨でしょう。 Tomorrow, it should be

rainy.

【あめ】candy
飴がなめたい。　I'd like to eat candy.

【あらう】to wash
ご飯の前に手を洗いましょう。　Before eating, let's wash our hands.

【ある】to exist
そこにトラックがある。There is a truck there.

【あるく】to walk
この子は、１２ヶ月で歩くようになりました。
That child started walking at twelve months.

【あれ】that
あれがほしい。　I'd like that.

Chapter 2

(い)

【いい/よい】　Good

まことは、いい子だ。（よいこだ）　Makoto is a good child.

【いいえ】　No

いいえ、ちがいます。No, that is wrong.

【いう】　to Say

はっきり言いましょう。I'll say this clearly.

【いえ】　Home

家にかえります。I'm going home.

【いかが】　How about…

お茶はいかがですか？ How about some tea?

【いく/行く】　to Go

こっちへいく。To come here.

【いくつ】　How many?
りんごは、いくつありますか？ How many apples are there?

【いくら】　How much?
これは、いくらですか？ How much is this?

【いけ】　Pond
池にくじらはいない。 There isn't a whale in the pond.

【いしゃ】　Doctor
いそいで医者を呼んでください。 Quickly call for a doctor.

【いす】　Chair
いすに座ってください。 Please sit in the chair.

【いそがしい】Busy
今日は、とても忙しい。 Today, I'm very busy.

【いたい】　Pain
歯がいたいです。 My tooth hurts.

【いち】　One; 1
一から始めましょう。 Let's start from one.

【いちにち】 One Day; a Day

一日の初めは、朝です。 The beginning of a day is the morning.

【いちばん】 No. 1; the best

私は、一番になりたいです。I want to become the best.

【いつ】 When

いつかえりますか? When will you return.

【いつか】 Fifth (of the month)

5月5日は、こどもの日です。May fifth is Children's Day.

【いっしょ】 Together

あの夫婦は、いつも一緒にいます。That married couple is always together.

【いつつ】 Five

まことは、五つになりました。Makoto turned five.

【いつも】 Always

あの人は、いつも笑っています。That person is always smiling.

【いぬ】 Dog
犬が好きです。 I like dogs.

【いま】 Now
今、なんじですか？ What time is now?

【いみ】 Meaning
どういう意味ですか？ What does that mean?

【いもうと】 Younger sister
るみは、私の妹です。 Rumi is my younger sister.

【いや】 Show of disapproval or disgust
それは、いやです。 I don't like that.

【いりぐち】 Entrance
入り口は、どこですか？ Where is the entrance?

【いる】 Live; inhabit
あのおばあさんは、毎日家に居ます。 That old lady is always at home.

【いる】 Want; need
お金が要ります。 I need money.

【いれる】 Put (something) into

コップに水を入れてください。Please put water in the cup.

【いろ】 Color

その車の色は、なんですか？ What was the color of that car?

【いろいろ】 Various

いろいろな本があります。I have various (types of) books.

(う)

【うえ】 Above; up

上を見てください。 Look up.

【うしろ】 Behind

うしろにだれかいます。 There is someone behind (us).

【うすい】 Thin

壁がうすいです。 The wall is thin.

【うた】 Song

きれいな歌ですね。 Isn't that a pretty song?

【うたう】To sing

歌を歌いましょう。 Let's sing a song.

【うち】 House

ここが私のうちです。 This is my house.

【うまれる】Be born

あかちゃんが生まれました。 A baby was born.

【うみ】 Sea; ocean

海は広い。 The ocean is wide.

【うる】 to Sell

この本を売りたいです。 I'd like to sell this book.

【うるさい】Loud; noisy

子供がたくさんいて、うるさいです。 When there are many children, it is noisy.

【うわぎ】Jacket; coat

寒いので、うわぎを着てください。 It's cold so please wear a jacket.

（え）

【え】 Picture
絵をかきましょう。Let's draw a picture.

【えいが】Movie
この映画は面白いです。This movie is interesting.

【えいがかん】Movie theater
映画館へ行って、映画を見ましょう。Let's go to the theater and watch a movie.

【えいご】English (language)
もっと英語を勉強したいです。I'd like to study more English.

【ええ】 Yes
ええ、そうですね。Yes, that is right.

【えき】 (train) Station
駅の近くに住んでいます。I live near the station.

【エレベーター】Elevator
エレベーターに乗ってください。Please take the elevator.

【～えん】Yen

１００円 (ひゃくえん) 100 yen.

【えんぴつ】Pencil

えんぴつで書(か)いてください。Please write with a pencil.

（お）

【お～】　Honorific prefix

おとうさん Father　おかあさん Mother　おはし a Story　おちゃわん (rice) bowl　おみず Water

【おいしい】Delicious

おいしいおすしが食(た)べたいです。 I want to eat some delicious sushi.

【おおい】Many

まちがいが多(おお)いです。There are many mistakes.

【おおきい】Big; large

象(ぞう)は大(おお)きいです。 Elephants are large.

【おおきな】 Big; large (-na adj)

大きな犬がいます。 There is a big dog.

【おおぜい】 crowd (of people)

大勢の敵がいます。 There is a large number of enemies.

【おかあさん】 Mother

あの人がおかあさんです。 That person is my mother.

【おかし】 Candy; sweets

お菓子を上げましょう。 I'll give you a treat.

【おかね】 Money

お金がほしいです。 I want money.

【おきる】 Get up; wake up

今日、私ははやく起きました。 Today, I woke up early.

【おく】 Put; place

ここに花瓶をおきましょう。 Let's put the vase here.

【おくさん】(your) wife; Mrs.

おくさんはいますか？ Is the lady of the house here?

【おさけ】Sake

お酒は好きですか？ Do you like sake?

Chapter 3

【おさら】 Plate; dish
きれいなお皿ですね。 That is a pretty plate.

【おじさん】 Uncle; older man
ぼくの伯父さんです。This is my uncle.

【おじいさん】 Old man; grandfather
おじいさんの家にいきましょう。Let's go to grandfather's house.

【おしえる】 to Teach
日本語をおしえてください。Please teach me Japanese.

【おす】　　Push
このボタンを押してください。Please push this button.

【おそい】 Slow
私は歩くのが遅いです。I walk slow.

【おちゃ】 I want to drink tea
お茶がのみたいです。I want to drink tea.

【おてあらい】 Rest room; bathroom
お手洗いはどこですか？Where is the rest room?

【おとうさん】 Father
この人が僕のお父さんです。This person is my father.

【おとうと】 Younger brother
Aさんは、Bさんの弟さんです。A is B's younger brother.

【おとこ】 Man
男らしくしましょう。Let's act like men.

【おとこのこ】 Boy
男の子がうまれました。A boy was born.

【おとトい】 Day before yesterday
おととい、日本に来ました。I arrived in Japan

the day before yesterday.

【おととし】 Year before last
おととしから日本語を勉強しています。I've studied Japanese since the year before last.

【おとな】 Adult
おとなになったらなにになりたいですか？
What do you want to be when you grow up (become an adult)?

【おなか】 Stomach
おなかがすきました。I'm hungry (my stomach is empty).

【おなじ】 Same
あの人とおなじものをください。Please give me the same thing as that person.

【おにいさん】 Older brother
おにいさんと遊びましょう。(said to younger boy) Let's play together. [Lit. Let's play with older brother. Referring to oneself in the third person is often done when speaking kindly to children]

【おねえさん】 Older sister
おねえさんと歌いましょう。(said to younger

girl) Let's sing together. [see above]

【おばさん】 Aunt

おばさんが亡くなりました。My aunt past away.

【おばあさん】 Grandmother

私のおばあさんは元気です。My grandmother is doing well.

【おふろ】 Bath

お風呂に入りましょう。Let's take a bath.

【おべんとう】 Lunch box

お弁当をつくりました。I made a lunch.

【おぼえる】 Memorize; remember

日本語を覚えてください。Please learn Japanese.

【おまわりさん】 Police officer

おまわりさんに道をききましょう。Let's ask the policeman directions.

【おもい】 Heavy

この箱は重いです。This box is heavy.

【おもしろい】Interesting

この話はおもしろいです。This story is interesting.

【およぐ】to Swim

あなたは泳げますか？Can you swim?

【おりる】to Get off (train)

この駅で降りてください。Please get off at this station.

【おわる】to End

今日は、ここで終わりましょう。Let's end here for today.

【おんがく】Music

きれいな音楽が聞こえます。I can hear pretty music.

【おんな】Woman

あの人は、女です。That person is a woman.

【おんなのこ】Girl

かわいい女の子がいます。There is a pretty girl.

(か)

【〜かい】 Times...
１回試してください。Please try it once.

【〜かい】 Floor (of a building)
２階にあがってください。Please go to the second floor.

【がいこく】 Foreign country
外国に行ってみたいです。I'd like to go overseas.

【がいこくじん】 a Foreigner
外国人と友達になりたいです。I'd like to make friends with foreigners.

【かいしゃ】 a Company
会社へ行って仕事をします。I'm going to go to the company to work.

【かいだん】 Stairs
階段をおりてください。Go down the stairs.

【かいもの】 Shopping
買い物をしましょう。Let's go shopping.

【かう】 to Buy

おすしを買ってください。Buy some sushi.

【かえす】 to Return (loaned item)

本を返してください。Please return (my) book.

【かえる】 to go back (home)

家にかえります。I'm going home.

【かお】 Face

顔が見えません。I can't see (your) face.

【かかる】 Take (time/money)

時間がかかる。It will take time.

【かぎ】 Key

出かけるときは、鍵をかけてください。When you go out, please lock the door.

【かく】 Write

きれいな字をかきましょう。Let's write with neat letters.

【がくせい】 Student
私は、日本語を勉強している学生です。I'm a student who is studying Japanese.

【〜かげつ】 Months
１ヶ月学校をやすみます。I'm taking a break from school for a month.

【かける】 Put on (one's eyeglasses)
めがねをかける。To put on glasses.

【かける】 Call
電話をかける。 To make a call.

【かさ】　Umbrella
雨が降ってきたので、かさをさしましょう。It has started to rain, so let's open the umbrella.

【かす】 Lend
本をかしてください。Please lend me your book.

【かぜ】 Wind
今日は風が強いです。Today, the wind is strong.

【かぜ】 a Cold; sick

風邪をひいたようです。Looks like (I've) caught a cold.

【かぞく】 Family

家族を大切にしたいです。I want to take care of my family.

【かた】 a Person

この方は、どなたですか？Who is that person? (polite)

【かたかな】 Katakana

かたかなで書いてください。Please write in katakana.

【〜がつ】 Month

1月、2月、3月・・・January, February, March

【がっこう】 School

日本の学校は、4月から始まります。Japanese schools start in April.

【カップ】Cup

このカップに水を入れてください。Please put water in this cup.

【かてい】Household

あたたかい家庭がほしいです。I'd like a warm (welcoming) household.

【かど】　Corner; edge

つくえの角に頭をぶつけました。(I) bumped by head on the corner of the desk.

【かばん】a Bag

あなたのかばんはどれですか？Which bag is yours?

【かびん】a Vase

かびんに花をいれてください。Please insert the flower in the vase.

【かぶる】Wear; put on (the head)

ひざしが強いので、帽子をかぶりましょう。The sun is pretty strong so let's wear a hat.

【かみ】　Paper

覚えられないので、紙にかきます。I can't

remember, so I'll write it on paper.

【カメラ】 Camera
カメラで写真をとりましょう。Let's take a picture with a camera.

【かようび】 Tuesday
火曜日に映画にいきましょう。Let's go see a movie on Tuesday.

【からい】 Hot, spicy
からいものは、すきですか？ Do you like spicy foods?

【からだ】 Body
体は丈夫です。(My) body is in good shape.

【かりる】 Borrow
図書館で、本を借りました。I borrowed a book from the library.

【〜がる】 Want, (wish, desire, hope) to do; tends to do...
あの人は、人のものをほしがります。That person tends to want other people's things. 人の嫌がることをします。(He) tends to do things to

upset people.

【かるい】 Light (weight)

この箱は、軽いです。This box is light.

【カレー】 Curry

辛いカレーが食べたいです。I'd like to eat spicy curry.

【カレンダー】 Calendar

そこのカレンダーを見てください。Please look at this calendar.

【かわ】　River

川が流れています。The river is flowing.

【〜がわ】 a Side

日本海側　Coast of the Japan Sea;　レストランは右側にあります。The restaurant is on the right.

【かわいい】 Cute

あそこにかわいい猫がいます。Over there is a cute cat.

【かんじ】Kanji, Chinese character

たくさんの漢字をおぼえましょう。Let's study a lot of kanji.

(き)

【き】 Tree

木があります。There is a tree.

【きいろ】Yellow

バナナは、黄色です。 Bananas are yellow.

【きいろい】Yellow (before nouns)

これは、黄色い花がさきます。This is a flower that blooms yellow.

【きえる】Disappear; go out

低電で電気が消えました。The lights went out due to a power outage.

【きく】 to Listen

私の話を聞いてもらえますか？Won't you listen to what I have to say?

【きた】　North
北へ行きましょう。Let's go north.

【ギター】Guitar
彼は、ギターが弾けます。He can play guitar.

【きたない】Dirty, filthy
部屋が汚いので、掃除をします。(My) room is filthy so I will clean it.

【きっさてん】a Café
そこの喫茶店でコーヒーをのみませんか？
Won't you drink some coffee at that café?

【きって】a Stamp
この手紙に切手をはってください。Put a stamp on this letter.

【きっぷ】a Ticket
東京までの切符をください。Please give me a ticket for Tokyo.

【きのう】Yesterday
きのう、彼女にあいました。Yesterday, I saw her.

Chapter 4

【きゅう】nine
まことは、九までかぞえられます。Makoto can count to nine.

【ぎゅうにく】Beef
牛肉２００グラム、ください。Please give me 200 grams of beef.

【ぎゅうにゅう】Milk
牛乳を飲むと、おなかがいたくなります。
When I drink milk, my stomach starts to hurt.

【きょう】Today
今日は、母の日です。Today is Mother's Day.

【きょうしつ】Classroom
教室で、みんなと勉強するのは楽しいです。
In the classroom, studying with everyone is fun.

【きょうだい】 Siblings, brothers, sisters

あの兄弟は、仲がいいです。Those siblings have a good relationship.

【きょねん】 Last year

去年からこの会社で働き始めました。I started working at this company last year.

【きらい】 Dislike

私は、にんじんが嫌いです。I hate carrots.

【きる】　Cut

きのう、髪を切りました。Yesterday, I had my hair cut.

【きる】　Wear

この服を着て踊ってください。Put on these cloths and dance.

【きれい】 Beautiful, pretty

あなたは、きれいです。You are pretty.

【キロ】　a Kilogram

体重が１キロ増えました。My weight increased by a kilogram.

【キロ】 a Kilometer
３０キロ走ってやせました。I lost weight after running 30 kilometers.

【ぎんこう】a Bank
日曜日は、銀行は休みです。The bank is closed on Sunday.

【きんようび】Friday
金曜日には、どこかへ食事に行く人が多いです。
On Fridays, there are many people going out to eat.

(く)

【く】 Nine
九九を覚えました。I've memorized the multiplication tables.

【くすり】Medicine, a drug
風邪を引いたので、薬を飲みました。I caught a cold so I took some medicine.

【ください】Give, please
お茶をください。Please give me some tea.

【くち】a Mouth

口からうまれたみたいに、よくしゃべる人だ。

It's like he was born with the gift of gab; (he) talks all the time. (idiom: born from a mouth)

【くつ】 Shoes

家に入るときは、ちゃんと靴を脱いでください。When you enter the house, be sure to take off your shoes.

【くつした】Socks

靴下に穴が開いてしまいました。(My) socks got a hole.

【くに】a Country

どこの国の人ですか？What nationality (are you)?

【くもり】Cloudy

今日は、くもりです。Today it is cloudy.

【くもる】Become cloudy

ちょっと曇ってきましたね。It has become a little cloudy.

【くらい】 Dark
部屋が暗いです。(This) room is dark.

【〜くらい/ぐらい】 About, almost, some
あの子は、3歳くらいに見えます。That child seems to be about three years old.

【クラス】 a Class
日本語のクラスは、ここです。The Japanese class is here.

【グラム】 a Gram
1キロは、1000グラムです。One kilogram is a thousand grams.

【くる】 Come
あの人は、きっと来ると思います。I'm sure that person will come.

【くるま】 Car
うちの子は、車が大好きです。My child loves cars.

【くろ】 Black
赤じゃなくて、黒のペンをください。Not a red,

but a black pen please.

【くろい】 Black (before nouns)

あそこに黒い車があります。There is a black car over there.

（け）

【けいかん】 a Police officer

警官が来ました。A police officer came.

【けさ】　This morning

今朝は、すこし雨が降っています。This morning it is raining a little.

【けす】　Erase, delete, put out (a fire) turn off (TV)

黒板の字をけしてください。Please erase the chalkboard.

【けっこう】 Fine, nice good

たいへん結構なものをいただきまして、ありがとうございます。Thank you for such a nice gift. (polite)

【けっこん・する】 to Marry, get married

彼女(かのじょ)は、もうすぐ結婚(けっこん)します。 She will get married soon.

【げつようび】 Monday

今日(きょう)は、月曜日(げつようび)です。 Today is Monday.

【げんかん】 the Entrance; (where you take off shoes to enter the house)

玄関(げんかん)はどこですか？ Where is the entrance?

【げんき】 Energy, vitality, healthy

お元気(げんき)ですか？ How are you?

（こ）

【〜こ】　a Piece, (a counter for objects)

りんごを5個(こ)ください。 Please give me five apples.

【ご】　Five

りんごを五個(ごこ)ください。 Please give me five apples.

【〜ご】　a Language

日本語(にほんご)ができます。I can speak Japanese.

【こうえん】a Park

今日(きょう)は、公園(こうえん)へいきましょう。Let's go to the park today.

【こうさてん】an Intersection

交差点(こうさてん)では、ちゃんと信号(しんごう)をみましょう。At intersections, be sure to watch the signal.

【こうちゃ】Tea, black tea

今朝(けさ)は、紅茶(こうちゃ)がのみたいです。This morning, I'd like to drink some black tea.

【こうばん】Police box

道(みち)に迷(まよ)ったので、あの交番(こうばん)で道(みち)をききましょう。I've lost my way, let's ask directions at that police station (box).

【こえ】　Voice

今(いま)、だれかの声(こえ)が聞(き)こえました。Just now, I heard someone's voice.

【コート】Coat
寒いのでコートを着たほうがいいですね。It's cold so it would be better to wear a coat.

【コーヒー】Coffee
コーヒーをお願いします。Please give me a coffee.

【ここ】　Here
ここにおいてください。Please wait here.

【ごご】　P.M.; afternoon
午後1時にここに来てください。Please come here at 1 PM.

【ここのか】the Ninth (of the month)
今日は、五月九日です。Today is May 9th.

【ここのつ】Nine
ひとつ(1)、ふたつ(2)、みっつ(3)、よっつ(4)、いつつ(5)、むっつ(6)、ななつ(7)、やっつ(8)、ここのつ(9)、とお(10)。

【ごぜん】A.M.; morning
これで、午前の授業はおわりです。We'll end this morning's class here.

【こたえる】to Answer
この問題は、難しいので、答えられませんでした。Because that problem was difficult, I wasn't able to answer.

【こちら】Here; this place
こちらにいらしてください。Please come here. (polite)

【こっち】Here
こっちにきてください。Please come here.

【ことし】This year
今年は、豊作です。This year has a good harvest.

【ことば】Language
この言葉は、どういういみですか？ What does this word mean?

【こども】Children
五月五日はこどもの日です。May 5th is Children's Day.

【この】 This...
このノートは、だれのですか？ Whose notebook is this?

【ごはん】Food; rice
おなかがすいたので、ご飯が食べたいです。
I'm hungry so I want to eat food.

【コピー・する】to Copy
これをコピーしてください。Please copy this.

【こまる】be Inconvenienced; troubled
お金がなくて、困っています。Not having money is troublesome.

【これ】 This
これはなんですか？What is this?

【〜ころ/ごろ】During (that) time
来年の今頃は、何をしているでしょうか？ I wonder what (we'll) be doing this time next year.

【こんげつ】This month
今月からガソリン代があがります。From this month, gas will go up.

【こんしゅう】This week
今週は、日本語教室は休みです。Japanese class is off this week.

【こんな】 Such; this; like this
こんなはずではなかったのですが・・・。It shouldn't have been like that.

【こんばん】 Tonight
今晩(こんばん)、おひまですか？Do you have free time tonight?

Chapter 5

（さ）

【さあ】　Well...
さあ、いこう。Well, let's go!

【〜さい】Years old; age
このおばあさんは、ことし１００歳になりました。This old lady will become 100 this year.

【さいふ】Wallet
財布を家に忘れてきました。(I) forgot my wallet at home.

【さかな】Fish
あの河には、たくさんの魚が泳いでいます。There are many fish swimming in that river.

【さき】　Just then; before
先のことは、まったくわかりません。About

what just happened, I have no idea.

【さく】　Blossom; bloom

桜の花が咲きました。The cherry blossoms have bloomed.

【さくぶん】Composition; writing

日本語で作文を書いてみました。I attempted to write a Japanese composition.

【さす】　Open (umbrella)

雨が降ってきたので、傘をさしました。It started to rain, so I opened the umbrella.

【〜さつ】(Counter for books)

日本語の本を4冊読みました。(I) read four Japanese books.

【ざっし】Magazine

小説より雑誌が好きです。I like magazines more than novels.

【さとう】Sugar

コーヒーに砂糖をいれますか？Would you like sugar in your coffee?

【さむい】Cold

今年の冬は、寒くなるらしい。This winter, it looks like it will be cold.

【さらいねん】Year after next

来年には、４０歳、再来年には４１歳になります。Next year, I will be forty. The year after next, I will be forty one.

【さん】　Three; 3

一、二の三で、飛んでください。 one, two, three, jump!

【～さん】Mr.; Mrs; Ms

かおりさん Kaori san

【さんぽ・する】to Take a walk

私は、散歩するのが好きです。I like taking walks.

(し)

【し】　Four

いち、に、さん、し 1, 2, 3, 4

【〜じ】 O'clock

今、5時になりました。It is now five o'clock.

【しお】 Salt

その塩をとってください。Please take that salt (container).

【しかし】 But; however

私は8年間日本に住んだ。しかし日本語はまだまだだめです。I lived in Japan for eight years, but my Japanese still isn't good.

【じかん】 Time

日本に帰るには、時間がかかります。Returning to Japan takes time.

【〜じかん】 Span of time

飛行機で１２時間かかります。 By plane it takes twelve hours.

【しごと】 Work

仕事がいそがしいです。I'm busy with work.

【じしょ】 Dictionary

辞書でしらべてください。Please look it up in

the dictionary.

【しずか】 Quiet

この公園は、とても静かです。This park is very quiet.

【した】 Under

机の下に本があります。There is a book under the desk.

【しち】 Seven

おおかみと七匹のこやぎを読みました。I read the Wolf and the Seven Goats.

【しつもん】 Question

なにか質問はありますか？Do you have any questions?

【じてんしゃ】 Bicycle

２年生のときに、自転車に乗れるようになりました。When I was in second grade, I learned how to ride a bike.

【じどうしゃ】 Automobile

自動車を運転できます。I can ride (drive) a car.

【しぬ】　to Die

人は、だれでもいつか死にます。All people, whoever they are, will one day die.

【じびき】Dictionary

字引とは、辞書のことです。A "Jihiki" is a dictionary.

【じぶん】Oneself

自分に自信がありますか？Do you have self confidence?

【しまる】Close; shut

この店は、夜１０時に閉まります。This store closes at ten at night.

【しめる】Close; shut

玄関の鍵を閉めました。Please lock the front door.

【しめる】Tighten; pull tight

きものの帯を締めました。I tightened (my) kimono's belt.

【じゃ/じゃあ】Well, then

じゃあ、またね。 Well, see you later.

【しゃしん】Photo

私の両親は、孫の写真を大事にしています。
My parents cherish their grandkid's photos.

【シャツ】Shirt

シャツを脱いでください。Please take off your shirt.

【シャワー】Shower

汗をかいたので、シャワーを浴びます。I sweated so I will take a shower.

【じゅう】Ten

まだ十人が建物の中にいます。There are still ten people in the building.

【〜じゅう】Throughout

そのうわさは、学校中にひろまりました。
That rumor spread throughout the school.

【〜週間】Week (time period)

今日から1週間は、学校が休みです。From now until a week later, the school will be closed.

【じゅぎょう】Class
英語の授業が、今日から始まりました。The English class will start from today.

【しゅくだい】Homework
宿題を忘れてしまいました。(I) forgot my homework.

【じょうず】Skilled; good at
日本語がだいぶ上手になってきました。(You) have become pretty good at Japanese.

【じょうぶ】Strong; robust
体は、丈夫なほうです。(My) body is fairly strong.

【しょうゆ】Soy sauce
さしみはしょうゆをつけて食べます。 Sashimi is eaten with soy sauce put on it.

【しょくどう】Dining hall
この食堂の定食は、おいしいです。The food from this cafeteria is very good.

【しる】 to Know
この人を知っています。I know this person.

【しろ】 White
その車は、白でした。That car is white.

【しろい】 White (before nouns)
白い猫がいます。There is a white cat.

【～じん】 (Counter for people)
私は、アメリカ人です。 I am an American.

【しんぶん】 Newspaper
私は、朝必ず新聞を読みます。I always read the newspaper each morning.

(す)

【すいようび】 Wednesday
今日は、水曜日です。 Today is Wednesday.

【すう】 Breath in; inhale; suck
蚊は血を吸います。Mosquitos suck blood.

【スカート】 Skirt
ズボンよりスカートのほうが好きです。I prefer skirts over pants.

【すき】 to Like

犬が好きですか？猫が好きですか？ Do you like dogs? Or do you like cats?

【〜すぎ】 Too much...

食べすぎには注意してください。Be careful to not overeat.

【すくない】 Few

パンダは、数がすくない動物です。The panda is an animal few in numbers.

【すぐ・に】 at Once; immediately

すぐに勉強を始めてください。Please start studying soon.

【すこし】 Little

塩を少し加えてください。Please add a little salt.

【すずしい】 Cool; refreshing

海の近くは、涼しいですね。It is cool near the sea.

【〜ずつ】 Little by little

少しずつ覚えていきましょう。Let's memorize

it little by little.

【ストーブ】Stove; heater

寒いのでストーブをつけましょう。It's cold so let's turn on the heater.

【スポーツ】Sports

どんなスポーツがすきですか？What kind of sports do you like?

【ズボン】Pants

ズボンをはいてください。Please put on pants.

【すむ】 to Live

この家に住んでいます。I live in this house.

【スリッパ】Slipper

家の中では、スリッパをはきます。Inside the house, I wear slippers.

【する】 to Do

勉強します。I am studying.

【すわる】to Sit

ご飯は、座って食べましょう。Let's eat while sitting.

（せ）

【せ】 the Back

彼は、背が高いです。He is tall.

【せいと】 Student

この学校の生徒は、優秀です。The students in this school excel.

【セーター】 Sweater

自分でセーターを編みました。(I) made this sweater myself.

【せっけん】 Soap

せっけんで手を洗ってください。Please wash your hands with soap.

【せびろ】 Suit coat

この背広は、私には大きすぎると思います。I think this coat is too big for me.

【せまい】 Narrow

この家は、狭いです。This house is small.

【ゼロ】 Zero
ゼロからやり直(なお)しましょう。Let's start again from zero.

【せん】 Thousand
千夜一夜物語(せんやいちやものがたり)(アラビアンナイト) 1001 Arabian Nights.

【せんげつ】 Last month
先月(せんげつ)は、休(やす)みをたくさんとりました。Last month, I took a lot of vacation.

【せんしゅう】 Last week
先週(せんしゅう)は、仕事(しごと)が忙(いそが)しかったです。Last week, work was busy.

【せんたく・する】 to Wash (clothes)
洗濯(せんたく)するものがたくさんあります。There is a lot to wash.

【ぜんぶ】 All; complete
全部(ぜんぶ)いっぺんに洗(あら)ってしまいましょう。Let's wash everything at once.

（そ）

【そう】　Yes; that is correct

青木(あおき)さんですか？はい、そうです。Are you Mr. Aoki? Yes, that's right.

【そうじ・する】 to Clean

部屋(へや)が汚(きたな)いので、掃除(そうじ)をしなくてはいけません。This room is dirty so I must clean it.

【そうして/そして】 And...

そして、夜(よる)になりました。And then it became night.

【そこ】　There; that place

そこに本(ほん)があります。There is a book there.

【そちら】 Over there

そちらに行(い)きたいです。I'd like to go there.

【そっち】 Over there

そっちは、雨(あめ)がふっていますか？Is it raining there?

【そと】　Outside

外(そと)を見(み)てみます。(I'm) looking outside.

【その】　That...

そのズボンは、穴(あな)があいています。Those pants have a hole in them.

【そば】　Next to

窓(まど)のそばに行(い)ってはいけません。You mustn't go next to the window.

【そら】　Sky

そらは、あおいです。 The sky is blue.

【それ】　That

それをとってください。 Please take that.

【それから】After that...

それから　どうなりましたか？ After that, what happened?

【それでは】Well then

それでは、失礼(しつれい)します。 Well then, excuse me.

Chapter 6

(だ)

【〜だい】 a stand; counter for vehicles

車は何台ありますか？ How many cars are there?

【だいがく】 university

来年から大学に行きます。 I will go to the university starting next year.

【たいしかん】 embassy

アメリカの大使館はどこですか？ Where is the American embassy?

【だいじょうぶ】 OK; all right

あなたは大丈夫ですか？ Are you all right?

【だいすき】 like very much
猫が大好きです。I love cats.

【たいせつ】 important
一番大切なものは愛です。The most important thing is love.

【だいどころ】 kitchen
冷蔵庫は台所にあります。The refrigerator is in the kitchen.

【たいへん】 very
今日は大変暑いです。Today is very hot.

【たいへん】 serious; terrible
それはたいへんですね。That is terrible.

【たかい】 tall; high
うちの後ろには高い山があります。There is a tall mountain behind our house.

【たかい】 expensive
このかばんは高いです。This bag is expensive.

【〜だけ】 only; just

もう一度(いちど)だけ。Just one more time.

【たくさん】many

この道(みち)はたくさんの車(くるま)が走(はし)ります。A lot of cars run on this road.

【タクシー】taxi

タクシーで行(い)きましょう。Let's go by taxi.

【だす】to take out; to send

ごみを出(だ)してください。 Please take out the garbage.

【~たち】plural suffix

子供(こども)たちが遊(あそ)んでいます。The children are playing.

【たつ】to stand

立(た)ってください。 Please stand.

【たて】vertical

それは、たてで見(み)てください。Please look at that vertically.

【たてもの】building

東京は建物がいっぱいです。Tokyo has many buildings.

【たのしい】fun; enjoyable

このゲームは楽しい。This game is fun.

【たのむ】to ask; to request

先生に頼んでください。Please ask the teacher.

【たばこ】cigarettes; tobacco

タバコは二十歳までだめですよ。Until you are twenty, smoking isn't allowed.

【たぶん】perhaps; probably

たぶんゴジラは本当ではないでしょう。Godzilla probably isn't real, right?

【たべもの】food

どんな食べ物が好きですか？What kind of food do you like?

【たべる】to eat

毎日ご飯を食べます。I eat rice everyday.

【たまご】eggs

卵を買ったほうがいい。It would be better to buy eggs.

【だれ】who

だれが来ましたか？ Who came?

【だれか】someone

だれか、助けて！Someone, help!

【たんじょうび】birthday

今日は私の誕生日です。Today is my birthday.

【だんだん】gradually

だんだん日本語を覚えてきました。I gradually learned Japanese.

【ちいさい】small

家は小さいけど、きれいです。The house is small, but pretty.

【ちいさな】small (*before nouns*)

小さな家に住んでいます。I live in a small house.

【ちがう】 wrong; different
それは違います。That is wrong.

【ちかい】 near
郵便局が近いです。The post office is nearby.

【ちかく】 near
この近くに郵便局があります。The post office is near here.

【ちかてつ】 subway
地下鉄で行きましょう。Let's go by the subway.

【ちず】 map
地図を持っていますか？Do you have a map?

【ちち】 father
父はアメリカに住んでいます。My father lives in America.

【ちゃいろ】 brown
茶色の服が好きです。I like brown clothes.

【ちゃわん】 teacup; rice bowl
ちゃわんを洗ってください。Please wash the

dishes.

【〜ちゅう】during; in the middle of

会議中です。In the middle of a meeting.

【ちょうど】just; exactly

ちょうどいいところに来ました。You came just at the right time.

【ちょっと】a little

ちょっと待ってください。Please wait a little.

(つ)

【ついたち】the first (of the month)

次のコンサートは来月の一日です。The next concert is the first of next month.

【つかう】to use

このコンピューターを使ってください。Please use this computer.

【つかれる】to tire; become tired

ずっと勉強したら、疲れます。If I study for a long time, I get tired.

【つぎ】next

次の駅で降ります。I will get off at the next station.

【つく】to arrive; to reach

やっと東京に着きました。(We) finally arrived in Tokyo.

【つくえ】desk

私の机は汚いです。My desk is dirty.

【つくる】to make

すしを作りましょう。Let's make sushi.

【つける】to turn on (lights)

電気をつけます。(I) will turn on the light.

【つとめる】to work; to serve

大きな会社に勤めています。I work at a large company.

【つまらない】boring; trifling

この本はつまらないです。This book is boring.

【つめたい】cold (to the touch)
氷は冷たいです。 Ice is cold.

【つよい】strong
今日は風が強いです。 The wind today is strong.

(て)

【て】hand
手を見せてください。 Please show me your hand.

【テープ】tape
テープがありますか？ Do you have tape?

【テープレコーダー】tape recorder
古いテープレコーダーを買いました。 I bought an old tape recorder.

【テーブル】table
テーブルで食べましょう。 Let's eat at the table.

【でかける】to leave; to go out
しばらく出かけます。 (I) will be out for a while.

【てがみ】(postal) letter

お母さんに手紙を書きたいです。I'd like to write a letter to my mother.

【できる】can; to be able

英語ができます。I can speak English.

【でぐち】exit

出口はどこですか？Where is the exit?

【テスト】test

昨日のテストは難しかったです。The test yesterday was difficult.

【では】well then, then

では、またね。Well then, see you later.

【デパート】department store

デパートで会いましょう。Let's meet at the department store.

【でも】but

デパートに行きたいです。でも仕事があります。I'd like to go to the department store, but I have work to do.

【でる】leave; go out

家を出ます。(I'm) leaving the house.

【テレビ】television

テレビをつけてください。Please turn on the TV.

【てんき】weather

天気が悪いですね。The weather is bad, isn't it?

【でんき】electricity; light

電気を消してください。Please turn off the lights.

【でんしゃ】train

最後の電車に乗りました。I'm taking the last train.

【でんわ】telephone

電話を使ってもいいですか？May I use the phone?

（ど）

【と】door

戸を開けてください。Please open the door.

【〜ど】degree; amount

気温は３０度です。The temperature is 30 degrees.

【ドア】door

トイレのドアを開けないでください。Please do not open the bathroom door.

【トイレ】bathroom; toilet

トイレはどこですか？Where is the bathroom?

【どう】how

今日はどうですか？How about today?

【どうして】why

どうして宿題を忘れましたか？Why did you forget your homework?

【どうぞ】please

どうぞ、座ってください。Please, have a seat.

【どうぶつ】animal

どんな動物が好きですか？What kind of animal do you like?

【どうも】(intensifier)

どうもありがとうございます。Thank you very much.

【とお】ten
八つ、九つ、十 8, 9, 10 ("native" Japanese counting)

【とおい】far
ここからちょっと遠いです。(It) is pretty far from here.

【とおか】the tenth (of the month)
十日に何かしますか？Do you want to do something on the tenth?

【〜とき】time
あのときのことはよく覚えています。I clearly remember what happened that time.

【ときどき】sometimes
時々、日本の映画をみます。Sometimes, I watch a Japanese movie.

【とけい】clock; watch
時計を忘れました。I forgot my watch.

【どこ】where
辞書はどこにありますか？Where is the dictionary?

【ところ】place
ここはいいところですね。This is a nice place.

【とし】year
一月一日は新しい年の初めです。January 1st is the beginning of the New Year.

【としょかん】library
図書館では静かにしてください。Please be quiet in the library.

【どちら】where; what place
お国はどちらですか？What (where) is your country?

【どっち】which
カレーかハンバーガーか、どっちにしますか？Which would you like? Curry or hamburger?

【とても】very

彼女はとてもきれいな人です。She is a very beautiful person.

【どなた】who (polite)

どなたですか？Who are you (polite)?

【となり】next to

ビルさんはとなりに住んでいます。Bill lives next door.

【どの】which

どの人が好きですか？Which person do you like?

【とぶ】to fly

スーパーマンのように飛びたいです。I want to fly like Superman.

【とまる】to stop

時計が止まりました。My watch (clock) stopped.

【ともだち】friend

友達になりました。We became friends.

【どようび】Saturday
土曜日は、家でゆっくりします。I will stay home (and take it easy) on Saturday.

【とり】bird
この鳥はどんな鳥ですか？What kind of bird is this bird?

【とりにく】chicken (food)
鶏肉を食べたいですか？Do you want to eat chicken?

【とる】to take; to grab
好きなものを取ってください。Please take what you like.

【とる】to take (a picture)
写真をよく撮ります。I often take pictures.

【どれ】which
どれがいいですか？Which is good (would you like)?

【どんな】what (kind of)

どんな食べ物が好きですか？What kind of food do you like?

（な）

【ない】none

私はスポーツには興味がない。I have no interest in sports.

【ナイフ】knife

パンを切りたいのですが、ナイフがありますか？I'd like to cut the bread. Do you have a knife?

【なか】middle; center

家の中に入りました。(He) entered the house.

【ながい】long

アマゾンは長い川です。The Amazon is a long river.

【〜ながら】while

食べながら、本を読みます。(I) read a book while eating.

【なく】to cry; to sing (birds)

あの鳥はきれいに鳴きます。That bird is singing beautifully.

【なくす】to lose (something)
かぎをなくしてしまいました。I lost my keys.

【なぜ】why
なぜここに来ましたか？Why did you come here?

【なつ】summer
夏は暑いです。Summer is hot.

【なつやすみ】summer vacation
夏休みには何をしますか？What will you do for Summer Vacation?

【〜など】and so forth
フルーツはりんご、バナナ、オレンジなどが好きです。As for fruits, I like apples, bananas, oranges, etc.

【ななつ】seven
五つ、六つ、七つ 5, 6, 7 ("native" Japanese counting)

【なに】what

これは何？What is this?

【なん】what (before other words)

紙は、何枚ほしい？How many pieces of paper do you want?

【なのか】the seventh (of the month)

ごみの日は七日です。Garbage pickup day is the seventh.

【なまえ】name

お名前は何ですか？What is your name?

【ならう】to learn; to study

琴を習います。I'm learning (to play) the koto.

【ならぶ】to line up

この列に並んでください。Please get in this line.

【ならべる】to arrange (things); put in order

子供がおもちゃをきれいに並べます。The children lined up their toys neatly.

【なる】 **to become**
春(はる)になりました。It has become Spring.

【なん〜】 **how many…**
兄弟(きょうだい)は何人(なんにん)ですか？How many brothers (and sisters) do you have?

(に)

【に】 **two**
一(いち)、二(に)、三(さん) 1, 2, 3 ("Chinese" counting)

【にぎやか】 **lively; cheerful**
このパーティーはにぎやかです。This party is lively.

【にく】 **meat**
今日(きょう)は肉(にく)を食(た)べたくないです。I don't want to eat meat today.

【にし】 **west**
太陽(たいよう)は西(にし)に沈(しず)みます。The sun sets in the west.

【〜にち】 **day**
一日(ついたち)で全部(ぜんぶ)終わりました。 I finished it in one

day.

【にちようび】Sunday

日曜日、海岸に行きたい。 I want to go to the beach on Sunday.

【にもつ】baggage; luggage

荷物が多い。 (I) have a lot of baggage.

【ニュース】news

最近ニュースを見てない。 (I) haven't watched the news recently.

【にわ】garden

庭にきれいな花があります。 There is a pretty flower in the garden.

【〜にん】people

何人来ますか？ How many people will come?

(ぬ)

【ぬぐ】to take off (clothes)

シャツを脱ぎました。 (I) took off my shirt.

【ぬるい】 lukewarm (not hot enough)

ぬるま湯で手を洗ってください。Wash your hands in lukewarm water.

（ね）
【ネクタイ】 necktie

毎朝、ネクタイをします。Every morning, I put on a tie.

【ねこ】 cat

猫が好きです。I like cats.

【ねる】 to sleep

もう遅いので、寝ましょう。It's getting late; let's go to bed.

【〜ねん】 year

今年は、２００８年です。This year is 2008.

Chapter 7

（の）

【ノート】 **notebook**
ノートに書いておきました。 I wrote (it) in a notebook.

【のぼる】 **to climb (mountain)**
山に登ります。(I) climb mountains.

【のみもの】 **a drink**
飲み物がほしいです。 I'd like a drink.

【のむ】 **to drink**
水を飲みましょう。 Let's drink some water.

【のる】 **to ride**
車に乗ってください。 Get in the car.

（は）

【は】tooth

歯が痛いです。My tooth hurts.

【パーティー】party

パーティーに行きましょう。 Let's go to the party.

【はい】yes; all right

はい、そうです。 Yes, that is right.

【～はい】counter for cups (of drinks)

ごはんを２杯食べました I ate two cups of rice.

【はいざら】ashtray

灰皿をとってください。Please take the ashtray away.

【はいる】to enter

家に入ってください。Please enter the house.

【はがき】post card

はがきを出してください。Please send this postcard.

【はく】to put (shoes) on
靴を履いてください。Put on shoes.

【はこ】box
箱を開けてください。Open the box.

【はし】bridge
橋を渡りましょう。Let's cross the bridge.

【はし】chopsticks
はしを使えますか？Can you use chopsticks?

【はじまる】to begin; to start
それでは、授業を始めましょう。Well then, let's start the class.

【はじめに】in the beginning; at the start
初めに英語を勉強しましょう。Let's first study English.

【はじめて】the first
初めて車を運転しました。I drove a car for the first time.

【はしる】to run

あそこまで走ってみましょう。Let's try to run to over there.

【バス】bus

バスで行きましょう。Let's go by bus.

【バター】butter

パンにバターを塗りましょう。Spread butter on the bread.

【はたち】twenty years old

日本では、二十歳で大人です。In Japan, a person is an adult at twenty.

【はたらく】to work

毎日働いています。(I) work every day.

【はち】eight

六、七、八 6, 7, 8 ("Chinese" counting)

【はつか】the twentieth (of the month)

今日は、六月二十日です。Today is June twentieth.

【はな】flower

この花はいいにおいがします。This flower has a nice smell.

【はな】nose

ぞうの鼻は長いです。 The elephant's nose is long.

【はなし】story; talk

あなたの話はおもしろいです。Your story (telling) is interesting.

【はなす】to talk

あの子はよく話します。That child talks a lot.

【はは】mother

母にプレゼントをあげました。I gave my mother a present.

【はやい】fast; early

朝早く起きて、新聞を読みます。I wake up early and read the newspaper.

【はやい】fast

あのランナーは速い。That runner is fast.

【はる】 Spring
春が一番好きです。I like Spring the best.

【はる】 to paste; to stick
切手をはってください。Please put a stamp (on it).

【はれ】 sunny; fair weather
今日の天気は晴れです。Today's weather is nice.

【はれる】 clear up (weather)
午後から晴れるでしょう。It is supposed to clear up this afternoon.

【はん】 half
一時間半かかりました。It will take an hour and a half.

【ばん】 evening; night
今晩は忙しいですか？Are you busy tonight?

【〜ばん】 number (counter)
競走で二番になりました。In a race, I came in second.

【パン】bread

どんなパンが好きですか？What kind of bread do you like?

【ハンカチ】handkerchief

ハンカチを持っていますか？Do you have a handkerchief?

【ばんごう】number

あなたの電話番号を教えてください。Please tell me your phone number.

【ばんごはん】supper

晩御飯は何がいい？What would you like for supper?

【はんぶん】half

ケーキの半分食べました。I ate half of the cake.

(ひ)

【ひがし】east

東京は東にあります。Tokyo is in the east.

【～ひき】(counter for animals)
猫は何匹いますか？How many cats are there?

【ひく】to pull
カーテンを引いてください。Please pull the curtain.

【ひく】to play (music instruments)
子供のころからピアノを弾いていました。I've played piano since childhood.

【ひくい】low
天井が低いので、気をつけて。The ceiling is low, so please be careful.

【ひこうき】plane
飛行機で日本に行きました。I went to Japan by plane.

【ひだり】left
私の家は左にあります。My house is on the left.

【ひと】person
あの人はだれですか？Who is that person?

87

【ひとつ】one
一つのりんごをください。Please give me one apple.

【ひとつき】one month
一月の給料 A month's salary.

【ひとり】alone (one person)
一人の女の人が来ました。One woman came.

【ひま】free time
今、暇ですか？Do you have free time now?

【ひゃく】a hundred
百円を持っていますか？Do you have 100 yen?

【びょういん】hospital
病院で友達に会いました。I saw a friend at the hospital.

【びょうき】sickness
ちょっと病気です。I am a little sick.

【ひらがな】hiragana
ひらがなが分かりますか？Do you know

hiragana?

【ひる】noon
昼からは忙しいです。I will be busy from noon.

【ひるごはん】lunch
昼ごはんは何にしましたか？What did you have for lunch?

【ひろい】wide
海は広いです。The ocean is wide.

(ふ)

【フィルム】film
デジカメはフィルムがいりません。A digital camera doesn't need film.

【ふうとう】envelope
手紙を封筒に入れます。(I) put a letter in an envelope.

【プール】pool
夏にはプールで遊ぶのが楽しいです。Playing at a pool in the summer is fun.

【フォーク】fork

フォークかはしか、どっちが使いたいですか？
Which would you like to use, a fork or chopsticks?

【ふく】to blow

いい風が吹きます。A nice breeze is blowing.

【ふく】clothes

どんな服が好きですか？What kind of clothes do you like?

【ふたつ】two

一つ、二つ、三つ 1, 2, 3 ("native" Japanese counting)

【ぶたにく】pork

豚肉を食べますか？ Do you eat pork?

【ふたり】two people

あの二人はいつも一緒です。Those two are always together.

【ふつか】the second (of the month)

二日が金曜日です。The second is a Friday.

【ふとい】fat; thick

この木はとても太いです。This tree is very thick.

【ふゆ】winter

日本の冬はとても寒いです。Winter in Japan is very cold.

【ふる】to fall (rain)

今日は雨が降りました。It rained today.

【ふるい】old

彼は古い服が好きです。He likes old clothes.

【ふろ】bath

今日はまだ風呂にはいっていないです。I haven't taken a bath yet today.

【～ふん】minute

何分かかりますか？How many minutes will it take?

【ぶんしょう】a writing; composition

英語の文章を読みます。I am reading an English composition.

（へ）

【ページ】page
次のページに行きましょう。Let's go to the next page.

【へた】poor; not good at
野球は好きですけど、下手です。I like baseball, but I'm not good at it.

【ベッド】bed
ベッドがやわらかいです。(My) bed is soft.

【ペット】pet
ペットがいますか？Do you have a pet?

【へや】a room
私の部屋は広いです。My room is spacious.

【へん】area; part
この辺に住んでいます。(I) live in this area.

【ペン】pen
赤いペンがほしい。I want a red pen.

【べんきょう】study

毎日、日本語を勉強します。I study Japanese everyday.

【べんり】convenient

携帯電話が便利です。A cell phone is convenient.

(ほ)

【ほう】direction

右のほうに曲がります。(I) am turning (in the) right (direction).

【ぼうし】hat

この帽子はどこで買いましたか？Where did you buy this hat?

【ボールペン】ball pen

ボールペンがありますか？Do you have a ball pen?

【ほか】elsewhere; something else

ほかのレストランに行きましょうか？Shall we go to a different restaurant?

【ポケット】**pocket**

ポケットにコインがありません。There are no coins in my pocket.

【ほしい】**want; desire**

新(あたら)しい車(くるま)がほしいです。I want a new car.

【ポスト】**postbox; mailbox**

ポストに手紙(てがみ)を入(い)れます。(I) am putting a letter in the postbox.

【ほそい】**thin**

あのひとは細(ほそ)いです。That person is thin.

【ボタン】**button**

一つのボタンがない。I am missing a button.

【ホテル】**hotel**

今夜(こんや)遅(おそ)いので、ホテルでとまりましょう。It's late tonight. Let's stop at a hotel.

【ほん】**book**

昨日(きのう)買(か)った本(ほん)はとてもおもしろいです。The book (I) bought yesterday is very interesting.

【～ほん】(counter for slender objects)

ペンを何本を持っていますか？How many pens do you have?

【ほんだな】bookshelf

もう一つの本棚がほしいです。I'd like one more bookshelf.

【ほんとうに】really?

本当にゴジラがいると思いますか？Do you really think there is a Godzilla?

（ま）

【～まい】(counter for sheets of paper)

何枚の紙がほしいですか？How many sheets of paper do you want?

【まいあさ】every morning

毎朝トーストを食べます。I eat toast every morning.

【まいげつ】every month

この雑誌は毎月出ます。This magazine comes

out every month.

【まいつき】 every month

毎月、家のローンを払います。I pay the house loan every month.

【まいしゅう】 every week

毎週、教会に行きます。I go to church every week.

【まいにち】 every day

毎日、新聞を読みます。I read the newspaper everyday.

【まいねん】 every year

毎年、冬には雪がふります。Every year in Winter, it snows.

【まいとし】 every year

毎年、フロリダに行きます。I go to Florida each year.

【まいばん】 every evening

毎晩、日本語を勉強します。I study Japanese each night.

【まえ】in front of

みんなの前で話してください。Please speak in front of everyone.

【〜まえ】before

一か月前、友達が来ました。A friend came a month ago.

【まがる】to bend

この道はよく曲がっています。This road bends a lot.

【まずい】not good; unsavory

昨日のカレーはまずかった。Yesterday's curry wasn't very good.

Chapter 8

【また】again

その犬はまた来ました。That dog came by again.

【まだ】not yet

まだ上手ではありません。I'm still not good.

【まち】town

この町の名前は何ですか？What is the name of this town?

【まつ】to wait

ここでちょっと待ってください。Please wait here a little.

【まっすぐ】straight

まっすぐに行きます。(I'm) going straight.

【マッチ】 **match**

マッチは木でできています。Matches are made from wood.

【まど】 **window**

窓から牛が見えます。(I) can see a cow from the window.

【まるい】 **round**

地球は丸いです。The earth is round.

【まるい】 **round**

円い大きな目。A large, round eye.

【まん】 **10,000**

日本語で一万まで数えられます。I can count to 10,000 in Japanese.

【まんねんひつ】 **a fountain pen**

万年筆がありますか？Do you have a fountain pen?

（み）

【みがく】 **to brush; polish**

歯を磨きます。(I) am brushing my teeth.

【みぎ】right
パン屋さんが右にあります。There is a bakery to the right.

【みじかい】short
このベルトは、短いです。This belt is short.

【みず】water
この山の水は、おいしいです。This mountain water is delicious.

【みせ】store
店でパンを買いました。I bought bread at the store.

【みせる】to show
見せたいものがあります。I have something to show you.

【みち】road
この道はどこに行きますか？Where does this road go?

【みっか】the third (of the month)
三日は私の誕生日です。The third is my birthday.

【みっつ】three
一つ、二つ、三つ 1, 2, 3 ("native" Japanese counting)

【みどり】green
緑色が好きです。I like green.

【みなさん】everyone
皆さん、お元気でしたか？How has everyone been?

【みなみ】south
南のほうに行きます。I'm going south.

【みみ】ear
ぞうは大きな耳があります。Elephants have large ears.

【みる】to see
毎晩テレビを見ます。I watch TV every night.

【みんな】everyone

みんなによろしく伝えてください。Please tell everyone hello.

(む)

【むいか】the sixth (of the month)

今月の六日は会議があります。There is a meeting on the sixth of this month.

【むこう】to other side; over there

山の向こうに町があります。There is a town on the other side of the mountain.

【むずかしい】difficult

この本はちょっと難しい。This book is a little difficult.

【むっつ】six

四つ、五つ、六つ 4, 5, 6 ("native" Japanese counting)

【むら】village

あそこに小さな村があります。 There is a small

village over there.

(め)

【め】 eye

何か目に入っています。There is something in my eye.

【メートル】 a meter

このプールは１０メートルです。This pool is 10 meters (deep).

【めがね】 eyeglasses

私のめがねはどこですか？Where are my glasses?

(も)

【もう】 now; already

彼は、もう帰りました。He has already come back.

【もう】 further; more; again

もう一度話してください。Please say (it) one more time.

【もくようび】Thursday
木曜日にデートします。(I) have a date on Thursday.

【もしもし】hello (on the phone)
もしもし、アオキです。Hello, this is Aoki.

【もつ】to hold
これをちょっと持ってください。Please hold this for a little bit.

【もっと】more
もっとゆっくり話してください。Please speak a little slower.

【もの】thing; object
これは私の物です。This is mine.

【もん】gate
門が閉まっています。The gate is closed.

【もんだい】problem
問題ありません。No problem.

(や)

【〜や】house; store; shop
本屋に行きたいです。I'd like to go to the bookstore.

【やおや】a vegetable store; grocer
八百屋さんでにんじんを買ってください。Please buy some carrots at the vegetable store.

【やさい】vegetable
毎日、もっと野菜を食べたほうがいい。You should eat more vegetables every day.

【やさしい】easy
この問題は易しいです。This problem (question) is easy.

【やすい】cheap; inexpensive
今週は、りんごが安いです。This week, apples are cheap.

【やすみ】vacation; take off time
この店は、毎週の月曜日が休みです。This store is closed every Monday.

【やすむ】to rest; to take off time

ちょっと病気なので今日は休みます。I'm a little sick so I will take today off.

【やっつ】eight

五つ、六つ、七つ、八つ 5, 6, 7, 8 ("native" Japanese counting)

【やま】mountain

山に登りたいです。I want to climb a mountain.

【やる】to do

今日は、仕事をやります。I will do work today.

(ゆ)

【ゆうはん】supper

夕飯は何がいいですか？What would be good for supper?

【ゆうびんきょく】post office

郵便局はどこですか？Where is the post office?

【ゆうべ】(last) evening

ゆうべ、何を食べましたか？What did you eat

last night?

【ゆうめい】famous
あの女優は急に有名になりました。That actress became famous suddenly.

【ゆき】snow
今年の雪はひどい。This year's snow is terrible.

【ゆっくり】slowly
ゆっくり食べましょう。Let's eat slowly.

（よ）

【ようふく】western style clothing
デパートで洋服をかいました。I bought some western style clothing at the department store.

【よく】often
映画館によく行きます。I often go to the movies.

【よく】very well
よくできました。(You) did very well.

【よこ】side

車は家の横にあります。The car is by the side of the house.

【よっか】the fourth (of the month)

今日は、四日ですか？Is today the fourth?

【よっつ】four

一つ、二つ、三つ、四つ 1, 2, 3, 4 ("native" Japanese counting)

【よぶ】to call

いつでも呼んでください。Please call any time.

【よむ】to read

その雑誌を読みたいです。I'd like to read that magazine.

【よる】evening; night

夜、寝る前に必ず本を読みます。I always read a book before going to bed at night.

【よわい】weak

私は体が弱いです。My body is weak. (I am weak.)

（ら）

【らいげつ】next month

来月までに宿題をします。I will do my homework by next month.

【らいしゅう】next week

来週、日本に行きます。Next week, I'm going to Japan.

【らいねん】next year

来年までに１００個の漢字を覚えたいです。I'd like to learn 100 kanji before next year.

【ラジオ】radio

車でよくラジオを聞きます。I often listen to the radio in the car.

【ラジカセ】a radio cassette recorder

この古いラジカセはCDがついていません。This old radio cassette player doesn't have a CD player.

（り）

【りっぱ】 great; fine

さっきのあなたの態度(たいど)は、りっぱでした。The way you just acted (your attitude), was superb.

【りゅうがくせい】 student studying abroad

若(わか)いころ留学生(りゅうがくせい)でした。As a youth, I studied abroad.

【りょうしん】 parents

両親(りょうしん)は今(いま)アメリカにいます。My parents are now in America.

【りょうり】 cooking

あなたの料理(りょうり)はおいしいです。Your cooking is delicious.

【りょこう】 travel; trip

いっしょに旅行(りょこう)しませんか？Why don't we travel together?

（れ）

【れい】zero
零はゼロのことです。"Rei" means zero.

【れいぞうこ】refrigerator
牛乳は冷蔵庫の中です。The milk is in the refrigerator.

【レコード】record
最近、レコードは珍しいです。Records are rare these days.

【レストラン】restaurant
レストランで食べましょう。Let's eat at a restaurant.

【れんしゅう】practice
毎日、漢字を練習しています。I practice kanji every day.

（ろ）

【ろうか】a hall; a corridor
ろうかが汚いです。The hall is dirty.

【ろく】six

中国語で六まで数えられます。I can count to six in Chinese.

（わ）

【ワイシャツ】a shirt

私のお父さんはよくワイシャツを着ます。My father wears t-shirts often.

【わかい】young

実はビルはまだ若いです。Actually, Bill is still young.

【わかる】to know; to understand

この問題はわかりますか？Do you understand this problem (or test question)?

【わすれる】to forget

宿題を忘れました。I forgot my homework.

【わたくし/わたし】I, me

私はカナダ人です。I am Canadian.

【わたす】to deliver; to hand something over

彼にこの書類を渡してください。 Please hand him these papers.

【わたる】to cross

道を渡る前によく見てください。Before crossing the street, look carefully.

【わるい】bad

あなたのほうが悪いと思います。I think it is your fault.

Download Link

Please go to this website to download the MP3s for all the Japanese: (There is an exclusive free gift on kanji waiting there too)

http://japanesereaders.com/1036

As an extra added bonus, here is a coupon **for 10%** off your next order at www.TheJapanShop.com. Just use the coupon:

MATANE

(Just use the above word in CAPITALS; no minimum order amount!)

Thank you for purchasing and reading this Book! To contact the authors, please email them at help@thejapanshop.com. See also the wide selection of materials for learning Japanese at www.TheJapanShop.com and the free site for learning Japanese at www.thejapanesepage.com.

Printed in Great Britain
by Amazon